**Robbie Olson
Colors of Love**

All rights reserved
Copyright © 2024 by Robbie Olson

No part of this publication may be reproduced, distributed, or transmitted in any form or by any means, including photocopying, recording, or other electronic or mechanical methods, without the prior written permission of the publisher, except in the case of brief quotations embodied in critical reviews and certain other noncommercial uses permitted by copyright law.

ISBN: 979-8-89383-691-2

Colors of Love

Olson

Colors of Love

You can write any time people will leave you alone and not interrupt you. Or, rather, you can if you will be ruthless enough about it. But the best writing is certainly when you are in love.

-Ernest Hemingway

For her

entre nous

I.
longing

II.
loving

III.
lost

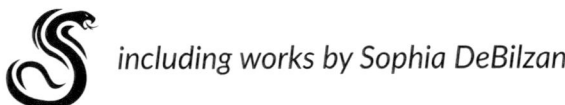
including works by Sophia DeBilzan

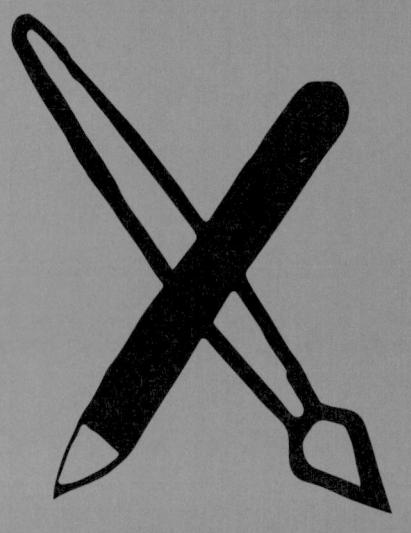

LONGING

OLSON

Myself alone again at sea
This time different,
this she
Follow my heading,
but at what cost?
Sail for paradise (I must)
or be lost

OLSON

In the dark,
Alone.
Waves crashing
Unseen.
Wind on sail,
    pushing me
        closer to her.

                The Sea Between

OLSON

So long awaiting a kiss,
never imagining the power
of a slight caress.
But just like the sea,
wave after wave
crashes without mercy.
Yet just the thought of you
keeps me sailing against the blue.
Risking all, small and great
For you, my one true fate.

OLSON

Again
restless sleep
Another staring
across
An empty
pillow

OLSON

No matter how great or small
the wave that passes by, I
send with each my love
in hopes it laps the shore on
which you lie.

OLSON

There's a hatch in my cabin
I can look through to see the stars
I hope you are staring toward.
If your head were next to mine
on the same pillow,
we could gaze together not
wondering about the other.

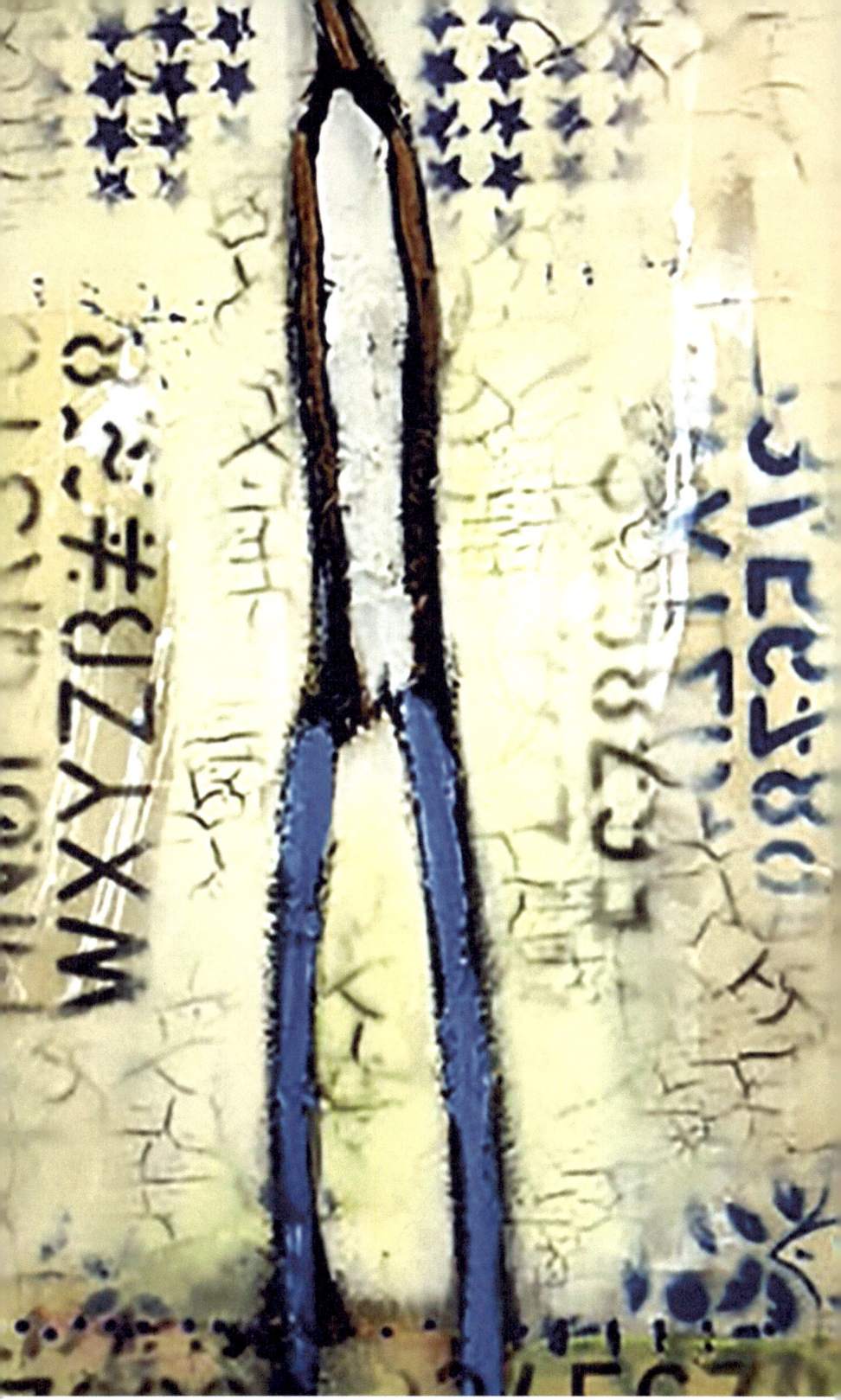

OLSON

A sea of colors
between you and me
makes no difference
with such embrace.
Rowing forward together,
Pulling oars to forever.

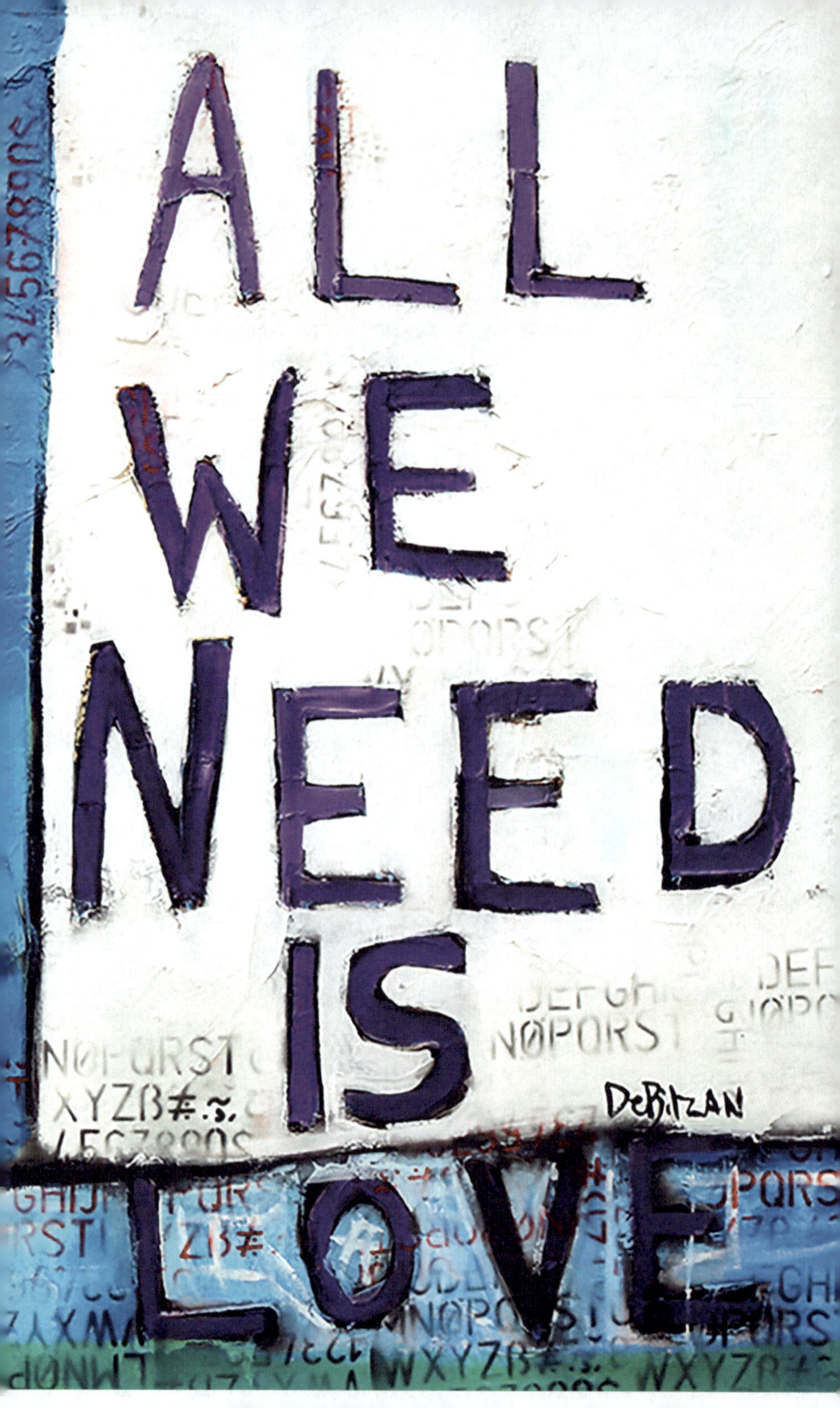
ALL
WE
NEED
IS
LOVE

COLORS OF LOVE

No mountains or sea,
nor things of this world
could keep us apart,
because this is not
my world...
you are

-Sophia DeBilzan

OLSON

How curious a thing that the distance
between us can slow time.
Never have so many minutes
stretched to so many hours,
only to become days in my mind.
Of course, there is no other
choice, I must go on.
It's just that never has so far
been so long.

OLSON

Hearing her
breathe
through
glowing phone
on my pillow
and she heard
me too
The way we
slept
not quite alone

COLORS OF LOVE

I hope you feel what I do
It is all because of you
I never seemed to be good with words until
you made poetry spill from my lips
(when they were once forced to be shut)
Nothing has ever felt quite this real
So I guess for now
I will keep putting pretty words together
to let you know how much you have my
Heart
And I will keep wishing
that I'll wake up in your arms when we're
Worlds
Apart
Because I'm in love with the impossibility of
Us

-I don't belong in this world
but I know
you belong in mine

-Sophia DeBilzan

OLSON

That first kiss
at first light
A beautiful ending
to such a night
was not the spark
of the love now grown
but the first taste
of a love long known

OLSON

I was

Lost, and
Only wandering; a
Void unfulfilled.
Empty

Yet you, with
One caress
Undarkened my night

COLORS OF LOVE

My love will always be right here,
where it belongs
in your eyes
in your soul
and between our holding hands.
My mouth hasn't shut up about
you since you first kissed it.
The idea that you may kiss it again
is stuck in my brain;
which hasn't stopped thinking about you
since before any kiss.
You're my reason to live,
and for that I promise to never let you go
until my last breath.

-Sophia DeBilzan

OLSON

What my life was
before you
I could not say

                              (i had yet to live)

OLSON

When I am
damaged, your
touches feel
like mercy

OLSON

From above
Heaven sent me
One Love

OLSON

Such a little soul
that's not
you
I have always known
your depths
have no end

OLSON

You laughed at me
that time I asked
"Whence you come?"
But we laughed together
when I had to explain
where from

OLSON

Floating lazily
I watched you
swimming in the shallows below
A dream in blue
until you came up
for a rum-scented kiss
Then down again
leaving me warm
in afternoon bliss

OLSON

One-eared bunny rabbit,
bearded dragon
and trippy troll-
shaped clouds
can only form
when I can feel the breath
of your giggles on my chest

OLSON

Are you a dream?
I don't want to wake up,
finding myself alone.
But fear the loss
from a slumber too long.

OLSON

Dancing all night
in bare feet
Tongues tickling
tasting sweet
And oh my
that dress you'll wear
when you say
I do I do

Just know dear love
me too

        Daydreams of Spain

OLSON

Together

our best poetry
is in the way
we hold each other

Close

COLORS OF LOVE

I remember once
that sound had a silence
But now
my meditative moments are
filled with
rhythms of you

-Sophia DeBilzan

OLSON

She came
Out of night.
Pulse quickened
Head dizzy;
Intoxicating sweat
Adorning her breasts.

Each time,
Always it seemed,
Took her one
Step closer to the

Blue swelling
Ocean
Of passion, swirling like a
Gale, waiting to
Escape her body in
Rhythms that
She could never have imagined.

OLSON

listening to her sleep
across the pillow
soft breaths
in warm rhythms
drifting off now too
dreaming until again
I can kiss her first light

OLSON

When you are next to me
I feel your warmth
like the summer sun
on my skin
So stay close
You know how much
I hate the cold

COLORS OF LOVE

My bones are filled with galaxies, and I will love
you until the stars burn out.
Maybe I could not save me from myself but
oh God
you sure did.
I guess it would not be harmonious without
a
little chaos.
So please,
let this be our beautiful catastrophe.
We only have this one moment, sparkling
like a
a gem in our hand, melting like snowflake
-I hope you like the stars I stole for you

-Sophia DeBilzan

COLORS OF LOVE

Nighttime tastes like you
and lately I have been starving.
You made me realize
that home isn't always a place.
Your arms are enough to make me feel safe.
And I don't know what my future looks like, but
I pray to God you are in it.
So let me discover the depths of your mind, because with you, I've lost mine.
I may not know how to fix myself,
but you put my broken pieces back together.

-Sophia DeBilzan

COLORS OF LOVE

Maybe it was the way you looked into my
eyes that trapped me
within the vortex of your mind;
your beautiful mind.
Show me all the parts of you that you've
been too afraid to face.
I've been dying for something vulnerable to
emerge from your mental escapes.
I'll run my fingers along your fears and
caress what you think are faults.
I'll show you everything you are,
forgetting what you're not.
I know you.
I've walked with you once upon
a dream.

-Sophia DeBilzan

OLSON

You thanked me for being a light
unto your darkness.
My love, I was only the moon
reflecting your shine.

OLSON

To simply live together
is an idea left wanting:
a view without the magic
only found in the living of a life
next to you and all the
                      steps taken together
      steadying stumbles
    discovering as one
Thank you for letting me see
     our world through your eyes

OLSON

My home
is in the rain
If where you are
is in the rain

LOST

OLSON

Dazzling glints on crystal blue
water
Relaxing softness of the
sand
Fire orange in the sunset
Comforting notes in my glass
of cabernet
Wonderment reaching down
through the night from a star-filled
sky
Just some of the things you didn't
need to take when you left

OLSON

This time I went too far
Sailed too close
to a beautiful shore

Tempted by a paradise
of real love found
Yet before a reach
ran afoul of ground

Wrecked and lost,
the wind now whispers
what I should have known
But ne'er could my heart resist
the chance to feel
and be un-alone

OLSON

The old lady selling vegetables at
the edge of the jungle asked,
"Where ya pretty girl?"

"Soon come,'
I lied.

"Go'on take two dem. Tell her one
fa fryin', one fa roastin.'"

Eating breadfruit for two days was
easier than swallowing the truth.

maybe it felt like
you lost yourself
because
your you
became that
part of Us

i know
because i lost
my me
when you
took that
part of Us
away

COLORS OF LOVE

I want you to tell me lies
to the questions
we could never answer

-Sophia DeBilzan

OLSON

that song
the words endure
emotions pure
but you left and made it real
this is not
Just like Heaven
and there is no Cure

OLSON

Like a drug too strong;
taken too much;
taken too long.
I went too far,
savoring ecstasy.
A fatal dose
ruining what was left of me.

But would that I again
swallow your taste?
I pray, Amen!
To die all over,
refuse, I could never.
No reason even caring
the comedown will last forever.

OLSON

Was it that I didn't say
I love you
enough
or too much?

I still do

OLSON

I don't want to tell anyone how we ended
awkwardly trying to explain why you left
I want to tell them how we began
How against so many odds we found each other
blended our souls
and lived as one

OLSON

With every sunset
my blues and yellows fade into
your purples and greens
disappearing over the horizon with
the setting sun
As I'm left in darkness
I hope at least you found your light

OLSON

Dreams like whispering
winds, stirring
memories of rustling leaves
strewn about the ground
colored with fading tinges of hope

OLSON

Those chopsticks we bought
because they were your favorite
color
Strands of hair in the back of the
drawer where you kept your
brush
The note you left on my pillow that
read
"I miss you already"

Just some of the shattered pieces in
a pile I've no desire to sweep

COLORS OF LOVE

Missing you comes in waves
And lately I've been
drowning
I can't tell if it is you
or the drugs keeping me up
at these abandoned hours
But I know it's you that is the most
addictive
A drug that pulls me down
to the heavenly darkness I don't have a
name for
The colors in your eyes are of an ocean
Paradise
Pulling me in like tidal waves
And now I'm lost at sea

-Sophia DeBilzan

OLSON

I found myself
turning to lift you up over
a puddle in the path,
but you were not there.
Then, just for a moment,
I glimpsed your reflection
between the raindrop ripples,
and stayed staring
at the wet mottled leaves
beneath my soggy shoes.

OLSON

I can still feel the softness
from the first time
holding your hand.
I wish had never
let go.

THE END

Based in Delray Beach, Florida, William DeBilzan is a world-renowned artist whose paintings, sculptures, and fashion lines can be found in galleries and stores across the globe. Notably, his works are featured in venues such as the Burj Khalifa in Dubai and the Marriott Central Park in New York City. Beginning as an abstract expressionist, today his work is immediately recognizable by his elongated figures, engaging textures, and rich color palette. DeBilzan explores themes of loneliness, friendship, and love, drawing on his own experiences while leaving his work entirely open to interpretation. He often conveys his love of the ocean and Caribbean Islands through the use of warm colors and simple compositions.

Sophia DeBilzan, daughter of William, was born in Santa Fe, New Mexico. Since that time, she has lived on both coasts of the United States, in the Middle East, the Florida Keys and the Bahamas. Growing up in and on the water, Sophia took the natural step to live and work aboard a sailing yacht in the Caribbean. There, her passionate nature led her to visit hundreds of tropical islands, become a master of the skills necessary on the decks of sailing ships, and cover nearly 15,000 nautical miles at sea.

From his early days, Robbie Olson harbored an unwavering passion for sailing and an unquenchable thirst for adventure. Originally hailing from the heartland of Ohio, he emerged as a captain and navigator of blue-water sailing. His academic pursuits earned him bachelor's degrees in both English and Fine Arts and a master's in Journalism, all from Indiana University

From left: Sophia, Robbie and William supporting hurricane relief efforts for the Bahamas at New York Fashion Week 2019

Once completing his education, Robbie returned to the sea, where he currently resides aboard his sailing yacht, S/V *One Love*. Calling the Exuma chain of islands in the Bahamas his home, Robbie continues to find inspiration in the unique rhythms of the ocean and island lifestyle

A portion of the proceeds from the sale of all printed copies
of this book will be donated to the following:

Staniel Cay All Comprehensive School
Staniel Cay, Exuma

Exuma Cays Land & Sea Park
Bahamas National Trust

Words, design and arrangement by Robbie Olson
Additional poems by Sophia DeBilzan
Art by William DeBilzan
colorsoflovepoetry@gmail.com

Follow on social media:
Facebook: Colors of Love
Instagram: @colorsoflovepoetry
TikTok: @colorsoflovepoetry

Made in the USA
Columbia, SC
27 September 2024